BOOK DESCRIPTION

In a creative project, are two heads better than one?

Writing partnerships can produce a remarkable synergy, building on each other's talents to create work unlike anything the individual authors could do alone. On the other hand, unsuccessful collaboration can be disastrous and has ruined many a friendship.

Kevin J. Anderson has worked on numerous novels and stories with dozens of collaborators, and many of those projects have become bestsellers and award winners. Rebecca Moesta has written books and stories with numerous other writers. In this in-depth book, Anderson and Moesta describe various collaboration methods with frank recollections of their own experiences. You'll learn collaborative techniques that will suit any sort of writer, as well as the pitfalls you may encounter.

This book includes a sample collaboration agreement to adapt to your own needs.

WRITING AS A TEAM SPORT

THE COMPLETE WRITER'S GUIDE TO COLLABORATION

KEVIN J. ANDERSON
REBECCA MOESTA

Writing As a Team Sport
The Complete Writer's Guide to Collaboration

Kevin J. Anderson and Rebecca Moesta
Copyright © 2018 WordFire, Inc.

All rights reserved. No part of this book may be reproduced or transmitted in any form or by any electronic or mechanical means, including photocopying, recording or by any information storage and retrieval system, without the express written permission of the copyright holder, except where permitted by law. This novel is a work of fiction. Names, characters, places and incidents are either the product of the author's imagination, or, if real, used fictitiously.

ISBN: 978-1-61475-655-2
Cover design by Janet McDonald
Cover artwork images by Adobe Stock
WordFire Press, an imprint of
WordFire, LLC
PO Box 1840
Monument CO 80132
Kevin J. Anderson & Rebecca Moesta, Publishers
WordFire Press Trade Paperback Edition June 2018
Printed in the USA
Join our WordFire Press Readers Group and get free books, sneak previews, updates on new projects, and other giveaways.
Sign up for free at wordfirepress.com

CONTENTS

Introduction	vii
1. To Collaborate or Not to Collaborate (Why?)	1
2. How to Choose a Collaborator (Who?)	16
3. Methods of Collaboration (How?)	30
4. Decisions, Problem-Solving, and Tips (What?)	59
5. Worst-Case Scenarios	80
Summary	86
References	89
Sample Collaboration Agreement	91
About the Authors	103
If you liked this book	105
Other WordFire Press Titles	107

INTRODUCTION

WHO WE ARE

Kevin J. Anderson, an international and *New York Times* bestselling writer, has more than 140 published books, over 100 short stories, scores of comics and graphic novels, and countless articles to his credit.

He has worked with dozens of coauthors, including his wife, Rebecca. His collaborators were chosen for a variety of reasons: because they had an area of expertise that would benefit a novel or story, because they approached him with an interesting idea or unfinished manuscript, or because they were close friends with whom he thought it might be fun to brainstorm and see what happened.

Rebecca Moesta, a *New York Times* bestselling author, has written or co-written more than thirty-five books, a handful of comics, and ten nonfiction workbooks, along with a smattering of short stories and articles. She has edited three young adult anthologies.

Together, we are Kevin J. Anderson and Rebecca Moesta (Anderson), a pair of *New York Times* bestselling authors. Not only have we been married to each other for over a quarter century, we have collaborated on countless books, short stories, and song lyrics. We also teach writing workshops together, and we're co-publishers of WordFire Press, LLC.

Considering the range of our experience in collaboration, it seemed only natural for us to write this book together, too. We hope our thoughts and experiences will help you become a successful collaborator, as well, and perhaps help you avoid some of the pitfalls.

ARE TWO HEADS BETTER THAN ONE?

Collaboration means working with someone else to accomplish or create something. It is an act of cooperation to reach a common goal.

Writing, on the other hand, is often a solitary profession, especially for those of us who write fiction. You've probably seen clichéd images of a wild-eyed writer, perhaps holed up in a cabin with no outside contact, staring in furious concentration at the empty page, with crumpled papers and torn up notes scattered all around. This stereotype holds elements of truth.

Most authors write alone, either in seclusion (e.g., a cottage, hotel room, or private office) or among people (e.g., in a library, the kitchen of a busy house, or a coffee shop).

There is no rule that says we have to scribble in isolation, though. If you find the idea of writing by yourself unappealing, there is an alternative: collaborate.

Some writers prefer to work alone, except for the company of their muse. Some don't like to talk about their work in progress, because they're afraid it might snuff out the creative spark. They don't dare to share their core ideas, for fear someone might steal them. Some are skittish about giving a draft to test readers, because they worry that it could deflate the entire project.

Other writers, however, are more social. They believe that ideas are not a limited quantity and trust that sharing can enhance rather than diminish creative energy. Many writers nurture their ideas under the sunlight of input from their colleagues.

If you're open to it and can be flexible about the process, your novel or story may benefit from having two (or more) heads instead of one. Writing can be a team sport.

CHAPTER 1

TO COLLABORATE OR NOT TO COLLABORATE (WHY?)

There are as many reasons to collaborate as there are potential collaborators. Later we'll discuss what to look for in a collaborator, but first consider why you'd want to join forces with someone else.

REASONS TO COLLABORATE

Enrich the Pool of Resources

Collaborating has the advantage of drawing on two or more different minds, areas of expertise, knowledge bases, sets of life experience, and publicity potential. Collaborators can produce a book that is unlike what either of them could have produced alone.

Let's say you came up with a novel or short story concept that captures your imagination, but you simply don't have the expertise to do it. No matter how much research you do, you just can't understand the life of a Beltway politician or an Afghanistan combat veteran or an abused gay singer. You might team up with another writer who has the knowledge you need and wants to help tell that story. The other writer may not have your ability to do worldbuilding or to develop characters or plot. But combining your abilities can produce a richer, more ambitious book.

Kevin says, "My first major collaborator, Doug Beason, connected with me at Lawrence Livermore National Laboratory where we both worked. We had each had some short stories published, and Doug had sold his first novel, a military thriller. I worked as a technical editor, while Doug, an Air Force officer, was a high-energy physicist with a PhD and had worked for the government for many years. I had a scientific background, though I primarily wrote adventure science fiction. Pooling our expertise, Doug and I were able to produce fast-paced, heavily researched high-tech thrillers in the vein of Tom Clancy and Michael Crichton. Doug had the military and governmental background to provide the veracity that those novels needed. I brought detailed plotting, worldbuilding, and action-writing skills to the table.

We wrote and published eight novels together through major publishers, as well as a handful of short stories. In 2017, we sold and delivered *Critical Mass*, a credible *Poseidon Adventure*-type survival story of people trapped inside a high-security nuclear-waste storage depot. The new novel incorporates our individual strengths as writers. We also drew on Doug's knowledge of the nuclear industry, his background as a former member of the President's Science Council, and his experience as chief scientist at the Air Force Academy, to infuse the book with a level of realism neither of us would ever have managed on our own.

Learn

There's no better way to learn different writing, plotting, characterization, and editing techniques than to work side by side with another writer and observe how he or she does it. How do they outline their stories (if at all)? How do they flesh out their characters? How do they describe a scene? How do they find time to write? How do they market their work?

Kevin says, "When I was just starting out as a writer, I collaborated with dozens of other new writers to do short stories. Many of those experiments failed, as you might expect, but I also learned valuable lessons about plot twists, brainstorming, developing an idea by taking an unexpected turn, alternating chapters with cliffhangers, adding emotion to writing. Reading a library full of writing books would not have taught me as much as working with a collaborator did.

Some lessons are vital, such as:

- There's more than one way to write a sentence or describe a scene.
- Your words aren't perfect, precious, or sacrosanct.
- A different take on dialogue or character might be more effective than the original one you imagined.

When developing your craft and process you can get set in your ways and think that yours is the only proper method of doing something. Collaborating with another writer can teach you otherwise.

Kevin remembers a particular "light bulb moment" with a collaborator:

"As an exercise, several new authors (including me) met together on a writing retreat to create a collaborative thriller. The plan was to hole up for a few days and bang out the entire novel, with each of us writing different chapters. In the lead-up to the retreat, we plotted a detailed outline with four separate storylines that all tied together. One of the participants wanted to develop each storyline independently, letting the events resolve in due course, unconnected to the other storylines. I disagreed, saying, "No, all of the storylines need to come to a head **at the same time**." One plot thread was clearly shorter than the others, and I insisted that we adjust the pacing to match.

"We laid out the plot on a bulletin board using index cards for our chapters, each card one of four different colors corresponding to the four storylines. I shuffled the cards around, demonstrating the impact and choreography as the plot lines culminated together like the grand finale of a symphony, which was so much better than having one plot thread culminate before the others.

"(A good example of this model is in Return of the Jedi where three main plot lines build to a simultaneous grand finale: Han, Leia, and the Ewoks are on the forest moon of Endor trying to knock out the Imperial shield generator; Lando Calrissian leads the rebel fleet in the big space battle attacking the Death Star; and Luke Skywalker faces off with Darth Vader in his personal battle before the Emperor aboard the Death Star. All of these storylines reach their climactic points at the same time.)

"I'll never forget the look on the face of the one doubtful collaborator as she got the concept and saw all the pieces fall into place."

Regardless of your skill level as a writer, there's always more to learn. Collaboration is an excellent way to bring new skills, techniques, and information to your repertoire.

Have Fun

For us, there's nothing more exciting than

taking an unformed idea and using another writer as a sounding board. We brainstorm together, developing stories and characters in ways that we would never do by ourselves. Plot twists come up that simply wouldn't have occurred to us before.

When Brian Herbert and Kevin plot one of their Dune novels, they meet together for days and just brainstorm, taking down notes, jotting down or discarding ideas then adding new ones, sometimes coming back to twists that now made more sense. He compares their collaboration and brainstorming to a jazz performance with two musicians—each performer jamming without sheet music, knowing his part, yet still able to surprise his partner.

Rebecca and Kevin work the same way. He says, "I'll take an idea and a plot outline that I'm excited about, one that I think is perfectly good, but once Rebecca starts massaging it, she pokes holes in logic that I hadn't noticed, builds up characters I hadn't paid attention to, and in the end it becomes a much better book."

The synergy and shared enthusiasm of brainstorming and writing with a partner make the process so much more fun than doing it alone.

Build a Career

Established authors sometimes collaborate with junior writers to offer them experience, exposure, and publication credits. In these cases, the established writer usually helps the junior writer learn the craft, provides a foot in the door, and sells a book that the newbie wouldn't have been able to. In turn, the newer writer does a lot of the heavy lifting of researching and writing the draft manuscript. We have both mentored many newer writers, helping them develop their craft.

Legendary science fiction writer Anne McCaffrey helped out many writers this way. She contributed her name to projects—often novels in one of her established series—and developed them with a newer writer. The newer writer did much of the plotting and writing, while Anne was there to guide them and to help promote the resulting works, many of which made the *New York Times* bestseller list.

Kevin says, "I've met many talented writers with impressive skills who were still trying to find their big break. By working with them, even on a short story, I've helped give them exposure they wouldn't be able to get on their own. Likewise, my own career benefits from the energy, enthusiasm, and work the other writer brings to the project."

Even when two collaborators are at similar places in their careers, they may help each other grow through the combination of their individual marketing platforms and fan bases.

Add Writing Accountability

Countless studies show that working out with a partner or group can significantly increase the amount of exercise we do, especially when those partners are encouraging. We tend to gravitate toward the habits of the people around us, so finding the right fitness companion can dramatically increase our likelihood of success.

Similarly, the right writing buddy can

- Hold you accountable
- Act as a teammate when you need help
- Act as a coach in areas where you have less experience
- Challenge you to stretch your ability
- Provide motivation and sometimes a bit of healthy competition
- Empower you

Make a Solitary Profession More Social

Writing can be a lonely business, so it's not surprising that the rates of depression, alcoholism, and substance abuse are higher for writers than for the general public. Staying connected to your fellow humans is a healthy thing, and collaborating can make the writing process more social. Look for someone you click with and care about.

The right writing partner can

- Provide a support system
- Offer encouragement
- Act as a cheerleader when you are discouraged
- Pull you back on track if you've gotten lost in the weeds
- Jog you out of writer's block, if need be

Increase Quality

Being part of a writing team automatically builds in one or more extra logic filters, pairs of eyes for proofing, beta readers, and editors.

PITFALLS, DANGERS, AND MISCONCEPTIONS
(WHY NOT?)

Thinking It Will Be Half the Work or Twice as Fast

Let's be blunt: this is a dumb reason to collaborate. If you work out the process and create an efficient routine, collaborators *can* get a book done faster than one writer alone. But when multiple people work on a project, don't assume it means you'll each end up with proportionately less work.

Even in a collaboration that proceeds smoothly, we each still put in about 90 percent of the work we would put into writing a solo novel—and so do our coauthors. Why?

For starters, there's more planning to do before you begin. You should make a written agreement that covers important issues, like how the money and credit will be split, what happens in cases of disagreements, disability, or death, and how to terminate the collaboration if one or more of the partners wants out.

Then, once you start the fun parts—brainstorming, outlining, and writing—there are more moving pieces, emails or phone calls, administrative details. There's negotiating and usually more rewriting. No matter how closely you work together, some disconnects are inevitable. For example, there may be details in your chapters that don't match, or you may want to approach a scene differently, or you may need to change a character's voice. You'll find a lot more back and forth.

Our close friends Dean Wesley Smith and Kristine Kathryn Rusch are a very productive, bestselling, and award-winning writing couple, and they've been together even longer than we have. They work on multiple projects, both individual novels and collaborative ones, some under their own names, some under various pen names, depending on the genre. They are so well-attuned to each other's projects, styles, and vision for the books, they can work together as a tag team to pick up the slack if one of them falls behind.

Several years ago Kris was in a bicycle accident and severely injured her elbow. With the pain she couldn't concentrate on writing (much less type on a keyboard) and the pain meds scrambled her thoughts. But she was under a very tight deadline for a Star Trek novel, and Dean was able to jump into the driver's seat and finish the work.

We have done that as well, leaning on each other to fill an unforeseen gap. But don't think that if you just pick up a collaborator, you'll write books in half the time with half the work. Never underestimate the horse-trading, negotiating, rewriting, and delays that will happen.

Losing Control

In most cases, for a collaboration to work, you have to allow someone else to tinker with your story, scenes, and characters in ways that you may never have thought of. Writing is a very intimate thing, and you are letting someone into your most private thoughts and words. You have to let go of your precious baby and then, after all is said and done, you have to split the money!

If any of the following situations makes you break out in a cold sweat and consider running, you may not be a good candidate for collaboration:

- Revealing yourself as a writer
- Letting another writer make changes in your plot or prose

- Letting another writer deep into your creative process
- Splitting the money for a writing project

Endangering Friendship

The sting of a failed collaboration can cause deep rifts. Writing with someone puts you in very close quarters with their imagination—and you have to let them into your very personal prose, too. You'll get to know each other very well—including all of your quirks, foibles, and flaws. It's like spending days and days driving cross-country together in a cramped car without air conditioning. Working as a team can throw a spotlight on the weaknesses of either author. Even seemingly minor disagreements can produce resentment that builds like steam in a pressure cooker.

We're aware of several close friendships that were shattered by an abortive collaboration. It has happened to Kevin once—and fortunately only once—with all of his collaborative partners, but it still stings a great deal.

So beware, and address potential pitfalls in

advance. Many friendships have been lost when the reality of a writing partnership fell short of expectations.

CHAPTER 2

HOW TO CHOOSE A COLLABORATOR (WHO?)

Before you jump in with both feet, think about who you are and who your potential collaborator is. Step back and take an honest look at yourself. What sort of creative spirit are you?

Finding the right collaborator is not unlike choosing a mate. After all, you are setting out to have creative "babies" together. Look for a person you can trust to become intimately involved with your ideas, your characters, your sentences, even your punctuation. This can be a daunting prospect. Consider not only the business advantages and disadvantages, but also the personal ones.

It helps if you're friends to start with, because you'll be borrowing each other's fictional clothes, seeing each other in what amounts to your literary underwear, and putting your heads together in brainstorming that goes deeper than casual conversation. Collaboration is also a business relationship with at least one common goal—the project. Kevin has collaborated successfully with people he had never previously met, but who were nevertheless the perfect person for the job.

How much you agonize over your choice of collaborator depends on what you intend to get out of the collaboration. Is this just a quick literary fling? A one-story stand? A couple of writers dabbling with a story to see if it works? Or are you looking for a long-term relationship? Are you committed to an entire novel? A continuing series?

Basically, the choice of a collaborator boils down to chemistry between the two people. You obviously want your collaboration to be creatively rewarding, and you want it to produce good work. It's also healthy for the heart and soul if you genuinely get along with the other person.

The more people involved in a collaboration, the higher potential there is for friction. Think of the collaborators that go into a band: drummer, guitarist, bassist, lead singer, keyboardist, and backup musicians (singers, strings, brass, tambourine?). They practice together, perform together, maybe write new music, and record together. Imagine the pressure cooker of being on the road with a group like that, driving from gig to gig in a run-down van, crashing in cheap hotels, trying not to let tempers rise. It's no wonder that so many bands break up!

By the time the Beatles called it quits, there were so many stark personal divisions among them that some members could hardly stand to be around the others. They squabbled about touring, support staff, their manager, artistic interpretations, production style, the direction of their record label, the influence of significant others, and which recording studio to use. Despite the interpersonal strife, they produced some amazing music on their final two albums, *Let it Be* and *Abbey Road*, but by all accounts, it was not an overly pleasant experience for any of them.

We'd like to give you the best chance at having a positive writing partnership. Know yourself, and learn about your potential co-writers. Here are some things to consider when choosing a collaborator.

WRITING STYLE: "PANTSER" OR "PLOTTER"?

Among authors, the divide between outline writers and discovery writers is almost as famous as the feud between the Hatfields and the McCoys.

As the name suggests, "Plotters", or outline writers, plan carefully, mapping out their book or story in detail before they write it. They may write an extensive outline, scene by scene or chapter by chapter, with character development, worldbuilding, and pacing worked out in great detail ahead of time.

Discovery writers are sometimes called "Pantsers", because they prefer flying by the seat of their pants. They start out with a blank slate and develop the plot, the characters, and the world as they write. They may begin with a general idea of their main characters or storyline, but feel more comfortable letting the details unfold as they work.

Each method is valid and there are extremely successful authors in both camps. (Full disclosure: we are both Plotters, and Kevin's outlines are very detailed, sometimes a hundred pages long for a 700-page manuscript.) Although there are many other factors in the success of a project, a collaboration between a structured Plotter/planner and a free-spirited seat-of-the-pants writer might not be a marriage made in heaven.

We know of one such collaboration that crashed and burned. Two well-known, talented authors decided to do a book together. One was a Plotter, the other a Pantser. Once they had discussed the story and the characters, working out what they wanted to write, the Plotter outlined the book chapter by chapter. With this roadmap in hand, the authors planned to alternate chapters. He would write the odd-numbered chapters and she would take the even-numbered ones. He wrote chapter one and sent it to his coauthor. She wrote chapter two. He wrote chapter three. Because he was on a roll and knew what the outline called for, he continued writing, completing several more of his assigned chapters (according to the agreed-upon outline) while waiting for her to write chapter four.

However, when the free-spirited Pantser wrote chapter four, she decided to go off in a completely different direction from the outline, killing off a character and choosing someone else to focus on ... thereby negating the rest of the outline. We talked to the Plotter, who expressed immense frustration. When his coauthor decided not to follow the outline, it rendered all of his subsequent (and already written) chapters useless. Later, the Pantser—who seemed baffled by her collaborator's frustration—said, "The new material was so much better, I had to go with it. How can he be upset with that?"

Not surprisingly, that book was never finished.

This isn't to say that a collaboration between a Pantser and a Plotter can never work. Pantsers and Plotters have complementary skill sets that, when combined, can produce stronger writing than either writer alone. It's important, however, to be aware of which camp you and your collaborator are in, then set clear guidelines (more on this later). That way, you'll know what to expect and aren't as likely to be blindsided, as the authors in the previous example were.

PERSONALITY TYPE

As an author, do you accept edits well? Do you take revision requests? Or is your work absolutely perfect in your mind? Can you go with the flow? Or is it your way or the highway?

As a collaborator, you and your partner will both need to compromise. In most cases, the work belongs to neither of you individually—you have to share custody. Are you able to accept that a sentence might not be written exactly the way you would say it, but is perfectly good nevertheless, as long as the story is good and the words are clear? Are you able to do as the theme song from *Frozen* says and "Let It Go"?

Are you (or is your coauthor) a diva, who thinks a sentence has to be written exactly one way, that there's no room for discussion? If so, you won't be a good candidate for collaboration.

In basic personality, are you both easygoing? Volatile and edgy? Are you reliable or flaky?

Is the other person someone you want to hang around with, on a personal level?

You'll have to answer those questions for yourself in each circumstance. The creative process is different for each person, and how your partner approaches the work might be incompatible with your own method. Talk it through beforehand and be honest with each other.

PROSE STYLES

Take a look at the writing you each do. Is your prose style distinctive, literary, flowery, or convoluted? How is your collaborator's prose? If one of you has transparent, workmanlike prose and the other has an ornate style, it may be painfully obvious that two different people wrote a piece. A style that might feel perfectly natural to you might be very difficult for your collaborator to match. One serious, one comedic? One light and lean, the other flowery and verbose? It might be hard to meld the two styles.

When Brian Herbert and Kevin chose to continue the stories in Frank Herbert's classic Dune universe, they made a conscious decision not to try to mimic Frank Herbert's distinctive style. Kevin and Brian's combined prose is clean and fast paced, and few readers have been able to identify which author wrote the first draft of each chapter. Although the language itself does not sound just like Frank Herbert, they remained faithful to the characters and the universe, creating novels with the same "look and feel".

When you work with a collaborator, going back and forth through the editing process, your joint style becomes a synthesis of the two. But the closer your styles are to start with, the fewer course corrections you'll have to make.

PERSONAL GOALS

Find out what each other's goals are. What do you want out of writing? What constitutes success for each of you? Your goals don't have to be exactly the same, but some goals may not be compatible.

If you hope to become rich and famous, but your potential writing partner yearns to produce literary art and doesn't care if the project ever earns a cent, you may be a mismatch. Or if you desperately want to educate and influence your readers, but your collaborator-candidate writes for fun and personal satisfaction and doesn't care if the project ever gets published ... again, probably not a good partnership.

Writers are complex beings and can have a multitude of goals. You can avoid a lot of misunderstandings if you share with each other what your main objectives are at the outset.

PUBLIC PERSONA

Are you the kind of person who is ready to jump in with both feet and promote your books to anyone who will listen, or are you more introverted? Do you have a platform for reaching an audience for your book? Do you each have a mailing list? A newsletter? An active social media presence? Or are you embarrassed when expected to give a "hard sell" on your book? Do you avoid posting anything online? Find out what you're each comfortable with. If either of you is reclusive, publicity may be an uphill battle.

SPEED AND WORK ETHIC

Kevin confesses that he's a workaholic. He writes all the time, is prolific, and charges in with a no-nonsense drive to get the job done. In choosing a collaborator, he wouldn't be a good fit with an artsy dabbler who daydreamed while waiting for the muse to provide inspiration for a line or two. He chooses writing partners who work as hard as he does and who write at about his pace.

Early in his career he attempted a collaboration with a well-known author, who had a much bigger name than his. It seemed like a big break for Kevin as a newer writer. Kevin asked why such a luminary would want to collaborate on a story with a lesser-known person, and the other author said he had noticed how productive Kevin was and wanted to observe his techniques. They discussed the story, came up with a good basic idea, and mapped it out into five or six scenes. They planned to write alternating scenes until the story was finished, with Kevin to do the first part. Excited by the initial meeting, Kevin wrote the initial three-page scene in a couple of days and shot it off to his coauthor. Several weeks later, the author responded with one page, the next scene. Kevin read what he had written, knocked out the third scene in a day and sent it back. Two months passed, and Kevin finally received sketchy notes for the next scene, which the author hadn't yet put together. The story was eventually stillborn because the two authors didn't mesh when it came to speed and productivity. The other author did, however, write him afterward to say, "Now I understand how you can be so productive—you *write all the time!*"

Brian Herbert, on the other hand, is almost as hard driven and prolific as Kevin is. After they outline one of their Dune books and split up the chapters, Kevin charges ahead in his writing, and Brian keeps up with him. Together, they finish the first draft of a substantial Dune book—usually 150,000 to 200,000 words—in only a couple of months and then dive deep into the editing.

Are you and your potential collaborator generally in tune? Do you both have the same work ethic and the same level of productivity? If one person is significantly faster than the other, consider making adjustments. Can the faster one take a larger share of the writing while the slower collaborator compensates by doing more publicity or research, for example? There are ways around even significant differences, but be aware of them beforehand.

WHO'S THE BOSS?

This is an important consideration in any partnership. We suggest that collaborators discuss it thoroughly beforehand.

If your collaboration involves ghostwriting, or intellectual property owned by someone else (often "work for hire"), or a Master/Apprentice situation in which you are not the Master (see Chapter 3), the primary decision-making authority almost always rests with the owner of the underlying intellectual property (e.g., Star Wars).

But what about when the authors are approximate equals? *Is* there a boss? If so, which partner is it?

In a worst-case scenario when the writers are at

loggerheads and can't decide which way to do a scene, who has the final say? Is there a referee? You want to minimize the chances for arguments and figure out how you'll resolve disagreements before emotions flare up.

We (Kevin and Rebecca) didn't resort to the "Boss" option, but when we disagreed, we split the decision-making authority according to our strengths. If our difference of opinion was about plotting or pacing, for example, Kevin made the final call. If it was about dialogue or character development, Rebecca's was the deciding vote. And so on.

Fortunately for Kevin, he and his most frequent writing partners—Brian Herbert, Doug Beason, and Rebecca Moesta—tended to talk out differences, listen to each other's opinions, negotiate and compromise, and come up with a mutually satisfactory solution. They never ran into a "my way or the highway" situation.

In one other collaborative team we know of, two authors collaborated on a trilogy for a major traditional publisher. Their credits were equivalent, so there was no obvious "boss", and they were on equal footing if a creative dispute arose. When they disagreed, they each argued their side, hoping to convince the other. If they still did not agree, they resolved to come up with a Plan C together. In practice, whenever this happened, they realized that Plan C was usually a better solution than either Plan A or Plan B had been.

CHAPTER 3

METHODS OF COLLABORATION (HOW?)

BROAD STRATEGIES

Collaboration strategies fall into three general categories: parallel, sequential, and interactive. [see References 1, 2]

Parallel

The work is split up by the collaborators, who then work at the same time on their portions of the project before combining them.

- Level Parallel—each partner participates at each stage of the process (plotting, writing, editing, etc.)
- Role-Based Parallel—responsibility is divided by function and then split among the partners (often used in nonfiction projects)

Sequential/Linear

- Single Linear—the team plans together, but only one person does the writing on behalf of the partners (works well for simple writing tasks)
- Sequential Linear—multiple partners do the writing, but one at a time. The first person writes his/her assigned section, then passes the project on to the next writer (and so on)

Interactive

Partners work at the same time, often in the same place, interacting with and adjusting to each other to develop and write the project.

EXAMPLES OF COLLABORATIVE STYLES

There are no hard and fast rules about the best way to collaborate with someone, since the "best" way is one that works for both of you. We've compiled a list of methods we've used or seen other writers use. (We named the various styles so that we can refer to them more easily.)

They won't all work for you. Consider them, try them on like new clothes in a department store dressing room, mix and match, or come up with something new. See what works best for your unique writing team.

Full Monty

What we call the Full Monty is a comprehensive collaboration in which each partner puts in the same amount of work. Everything is developed together. The efforts and responsibilities are split equally. The process is shared every step of the way. As you might imagine, this system involves a lot of work. It's also very rewarding, since the result is a true fusion of the skills and abilities of the collaborators. The end product is a book the partners could not have written individually.

Kevin recalls his early collaborations with Doug Beason:

My first Full Monty collaborator was Doug Beason. When we met, we discovered how much we had in common and quickly became friends. Shortly after that, we decided to collaborate as a lark and for the learning experience. No one taught us how to do it. As new writers, we developed the method ourselves through trial and error, and it seemed to work. At the time, we each had only a few short stories published in miniscule magazines.

Neither of us knew many other writers, although we had both met (as well as read and admired) Larry Niven and Jerry Pournelle, who were the epitome of a highly successful science fiction collaborative team. Niven and Pournelle had written such classics together as The Mote in God's Eye *and* Lucifer's Hammer. *Doug and I had no idea how Niven and Pournelle collaborated in a practical sense, but they certainly showed that it could be done, and done well, and done repeatedly. Obviously, Niven and Pournelle must like working together or they wouldn't have kept writing books in collaboration.*

Doug and I met face-to-face and talked about a short story idea, for fun: a space station is stranded in orbit after nuclear war on Earth cuts off supply lines, and a daring young astronaut uses an innovative solar sail to fly from one station to another to save his crew. We blocked out the various scenes in the story and decided to alternate writing them. We were ready to go.

That was when we discovered a large problem that modern-day collaborators no longer face: I wrote on a Mac and Doug used a PC. At the time, the two operating systems were bitter rivals who refused to speak to each other. When I wrote my first scene, I mailed Doug a paper printout, which he then keyed in and edited, then wrote the next scene and mailed the growing printout back to me, which I also had to retype to do my next section, and so forth. It was ridiculously tedious and inefficient, but it did let me study Doug's writing style line by line, and he did the same with my prose.

By the time the story, "If I Fell, Would I Fall?" was published in Amazing Stories *magazine, we realized we had a much bigger story to tell with that scenario. Doug and I got together again and decided to expand the story into a full novel,* Lifeline*. We* *met for hours at a time, brainstorming and plotting, developing the characters, taking copious notes, and building out the science, the space stations, the orbits, the solar-sail technology. The full novel featured three isolated space stations, a moon base, and Earth, each location with its own plotlines. The stories intertwined as the characters interacted and the stories progressed.*

For new writers, this was quite an ambitious task of choreography. We covered the floor of the office with index cards, each one with a brief write-up for that chapter, color coded by character (blue for one point of view, green for another, yellow for a third, and so on). It took many days of riffing off of each other's ideas, expanding on the scenarios, and rearranging the outline, before we got the story right. As we developed the storylines, Doug and I each developed affinities for certain characters. I wanted to write the villain, Curtis Brahms, icy and ruthless administrator of one of the stranded space stations; Doug was particularly fond of the moonbase commander, Duncan McLaris, a warmhearted man with a cute little daughter about the same age Doug's own daughter Amanda was at the time.

After we finally settled on the outline, we broke

it up into chapters. Depending on the characters we were drawn to, we each chose the chapters we wanted to write, dividing the work fifty-fifty. Lifeline has sixty-seven chapters plus an epilogue, so after some final rounds of horse-trading, we each had thirty-four chapters to write.

That was for the first draft.

We went off to our separate corners and each wrote our assigned chapters. Since the outline was detailed, and we had discussed all the events large and small, I knew what was going to happen in Doug's chapters without reading them, and he knew what was in mine, so we could work at our own pace. We kept in touch, engaging in frequent phone calls as we came up with new ideas, details, and twists. Neither of us got too far ahead or fell too far behind. Every so often we came up with a dramatic shift that would cause repercussions throughout, and we had long brainstorming conversations. Sometimes we talked ourselves out of the change, other times we agreed on exactly what we needed to do and which adjustments had to be made in the already-written chapters.

That was the easy part.

Once all sixty-eight draft chapters were finished —thirty-four from each of us—we assembled the pieces into one giant file. Thank heavens by this time my Mac had a way to convert PC files both ways, so we didn't have to retype all those pages! I was able to edit on my computer, and Doug edited on his. Then, one of us did the complete first draft edit. (In collaborations like this, you can decide who does the first pass by comparing each other's workloads and calendars or, all things being equal, by the flip of a coin.)

That stage of the writing is like carving a path through a dense Amazonian jungle with a dull machete. I got first crack at the rewrite on Lifeline. *I went through the manuscript, cleaning up my own prose and tackling Doug's chapters.*

Despite thoroughly discussing the details with each other, little differences had still slipped through. (This is inevitable unless you're psychically linked to your collaborator.) I fixed any inconsistencies I found and tweaked the scenes according to my vision of the book.

I smoothed out clunky writing—both mine and his. Even though Doug and I have very close writing styles, there were sentences in Doug's first draft that just didn't "sound" like me. I rewrote them so they read more comfortably to my literary ear. When it was Doug's turn, he went through a similar process to edit the book, revising my sentences that sounded clunky to him. My collaborations with Rebecca and with Brian Herbert use the same method. This first pass through each other's chapters can be a lot of work. Hence, our suggestion to choose a collaborator whose writing isn't dramatically different from yours.

IMPORTANT! I put that in loud capital letters because this truly is a key to a successful collaboration and maintaining a friendship. I suggest editing online, without using markup or Track Changes, so that the rewrites remain invisible, for you and your coauthor. I did not send Doug a manuscript covered in red ink to highlight every sentence I altered, every comma I added, every adverb I removed. And vice versa. Neither of us could see what the other changed, because that's just asking for defensiveness, arguments, and questions.

Handing a marked-up manuscript back and forth is akin to a teacher delivering a graded essay to a student. By changing a word, I was fundamentally implying that my coauthor's choice was "wrong", and that would quickly generate resentment.

Going into our novel, Doug and I agreed to treat each other as equals and trust each other as writing partners. Trust is as essential in collaboration as it is when you choose someone to babysit your children.

Doug let me rewrite his draft however I saw fit, and when I was finished I sent the computer file back to him. He started from page one on the second draft with the same carte blanche instructions. He could change anything he wanted, rewrite any sentence, delete any paragraph. I wouldn't necessarily know unless I went back line by line to compare—and I certainly did not do that.

If I wanted to change something substantial *in the rewrite, I called Doug to discuss it with him so he wouldn't be surprised when he had his turn. We almost never disagreed. A collaboration is a partnership. We negotiated, rather than put our foot down, although sometimes we grew quite passionate in our discussions if we held opposing views regarding a plot twist or a character reaction.*

When Doug finished his second draft, he sent it back to me and I did the third edit, which by now was markedly smoother. Doug then did the fourth draft, and we continued the iterations until we felt it was done.

No sentence sounded unlike something I would write, and no sentence sounded unlike Doug's voice. It was a perfect synthesis, and we sold Lifeline to Bantam Books.

Some of my Full Monty collaborations go through as many as twelve drafts, sometimes as few as four. Rebecca and I use the same technique, which boils down to

- *Brainstorm together*
- *Outline in detail*
- *Divide outline into chapters*
- *Divide chapters equally between us*
- *Write first drafts of our assigned chapters*
- *Meld all chapters into a single manuscript*
- *Pass manuscript back and forth for editing until it's done*

Brian Herbert is my most frequent collaborator, and we use the same method. So far we've written eighteen books together—approximately 2.5 million words in collaboration. During all of that writing, we've had only one or two disputes about the work in progress. Our imaginations operate on the same wavelength, and our work is a full, true collaboration.

If you can find a partner like that, this is a very gratifying way to collaborate.

Round Robin (a.k.a. Hot Potato)

Some writers prefer less structure, letting the story go where it will. Round Robin is an exercise in writing, rewriting, flexibility, and imagination. These collaborations are freestyle (or as we hikers call it, "going commando"). This works particularly well for Pantsers (see Chapter 2). This method is on the complete opposite end of the spectrum from the Full Monty above. Here's how it works.

Two writers decide to collaborate on a novel (which could take a lot of time and still crash and burn) or a short story (quicker and safer). They probably have some idea for a character, the plot line, or at least a genre. For example, "Let's write about a werewolf bounty hunter and see where it goes."

The first writer bangs out the first section or chapter and sends it off to his coauthor. The coauthor reads it, lets it spark some ideas, and writes the next scene or chapter, which she sends back to her partner. The "feral story" goes back and forth in wildly unpredictable ways.

Some authors turn this method into a game of challenge where one of the writers intentionally leaves the chapter on an unresolved cliffhanger or puts the character in a seemingly impossible situation. "Write your way out of that one, partner!" This can escalate of course, because once the stranded writer manages to resolve the situation, he or she feels obligated to end the next chapter with an even more untenable scenario.

This method can stretch your abilities as a writer. It's like being an improv comedian who is given a prompt from the audience. By the time this goes on for 70,000 words of a novel or 5,000 words of a short story, the end result may be nothing at all like what the opening paragraphs set up.

Round Robin stories can also be written by a team, with each writer taking successive chapters and rolling with it. The challenge of this type of collaboration is that it nearly always requires extensive rewriting. Someone has to go back and put in foreshadowing, make the characters consistent, add connections, and focus the plot line—especially if the story weaves back and forth like a writer who has celebrated a new book contract with too many drinks.

Another situation in which Round Robin

writing may be useful is when a writer has had a false start. The writer began with a great idea, but then the manuscript fizzled out. Maybe the main character became uninteresting or the plot ran into a dead end. Enter the new eager writer who wants to collaborate and says, "Let me see what I can do." The second author may take the false start and write the next section or possibly even complete the story. When one of your unfinished stories has gone to die, consider this as a method to breathe new life into it.

First Draft, Final Draft

Another frequently used technique between two collaborators of comparable skill and standing is for the authors to discuss the project, agree on the basic story, characters, and setting. Then one author writes the first draft, and the other author fleshes it out and does the final polish. The project is not always finished in only two drafts. Sometimes it still goes back and forth until both authors are satisfied with the polish.

First Draft, Final Draft is the technique we used for this particular book on collaboration. Kevin outlined the book and wrote the first draft while Rebecca structured it, edited it, polished the prose, and added material.

Kevin has also written novels this way with Sarah A. Hoyt and Doug Beason, and short stories with Mike Resnick, Kristine Kathryn Rusch, and Rebecca. This method is advantageous because it allows the writers to accommodate each other's schedules. If one writer has an opening while the other is busy, the first can write the initial draft and when the second author has time, he or she can take over the work and finish it.

Kevin and Sarah's novel *Uncharted: Lewis & Clark in Arcane America* was already sold to Baen Books, but when it came time to write the novel and meet the deadline, Kevin was swamped with two emergency deadlines and running a writing conference. He and Sarah met and brainstormed details. Then she blocked out the chapters and wrote the entire first draft, blitzing through. She's an extremely fast writer (and coming from Kevin, that's saying a lot). When Kevin had cleared his schedule, he took her rough draft and spent a month polishing it and fleshing it out while Sarah was caught up in another deadline. They are both happy with the end result, and it became a #1 bestseller in its category on Amazon.

We've each worked both sides of this method: as the initial drafter and as the final editor. For Kevin, the writing part is more enjoyable and the editing is more tedious (the opposite of Rebecca's preferences), but he can easily wear both hats, depending on what the project demands. One advantage to First Draft, Final Draft is that when one person writes straight through, the characters, plotting, and foreshadowing are more consistent. There's a lot less cleanup and rewriting.

For this method to work well, it's important to be flexible and to talk the story through beforehand to define the parameters. It ends up being a lot more work if you entirely disagree with what your coauthor wrote ("What was she thinking?"). If you end up throwing away half of the draft and rewriting entire sections, it's not an effective collaboration.

Follow the Script

Follow the Script is a variation of the First Draft, Final Draft method—a novelization of a story in another media. In this situation, an author receives a "first draft" that consists of the script for a movie or play. The author then adapts it into a novel. The script itself may or may not match the movie, but the owner of the original material (e.g., Paramount, Sony Pictures) decides how much freedom the author has in expanding the script into a novel. Sometimes, the owner only wants the author to add internal dialogue, along with descriptions of scenes and action that appear in the script. In other cases, the author is also allowed to add scenes, characters, and entire plotlines.

We have worked on several Follow the Script projects, both together and separately. We co-wrote the novelization for the science fiction film *Supernova* from a script (that was quite different from the final cut of the movie). We also did novelizations for *League of Extraordinary Gentlemen* and *Sky Captain and the World of Tomorrow*. In the latter two cases, only Kevin is credited on the cover, because that's what the contract called for. Rebecca knew this from the outset, and her name appears in the acknowledgments.

Kevin has also converted movie scripts by well-known authors into standalone novels. Dean Koontz, one of Kevin's most important mentors early in his career, wrote the script for a modern-day reimagining of *Frankenstein*. He liked his script better than the movie that was actually produced and felt it should have a much wider audience among his readers. He asked Kevin to novelize the script and build it into what would become a continuing series. Kevin enjoyed the work a great deal. The resulting novel, *Dean Koontz's Frankenstein: Prodigal Son*, sold a million copies in its first year of release.

Along similar lines, the publisher of L. Ron Hubbard's fiction wanted a new book. Hubbard, who was extremely popular with *Battlefield Earth* and his Mission Earth series, died in 1986, so there was no new material possible. However, in the 1950s Hubbard wrote a spy-versus-spy comedy movie script that had never been produced. The publisher hired Kevin to flesh out the script and convert it into a novel, which went on to become a *New York Times* bestseller. Using Hubbard's movie script as a first draft, Kevin produced a new "collaborative" work, even though the writing was done at a distant remove (since Hubbard was no longer alive).

Master/Apprentice

For the past decade we have spearheaded the high-level Superstars Writing Seminars, working closely with hundreds of ambitious new writers. Even before that we gave countless lectures and workshops at writers' conferences and science fiction conventions. We ascribe to the philosophy of paying it forward, so when we can, we offer writing advice and we critique manuscripts (please don't send us one!), helping to shape the next generation of writers. In this spirit, the Master and Apprentice method is a way for established authors to mentor up-and-coming writers.

In Master and Apprentice (or Jedi and Padawan, or Pilot and Copilot), a senior writer works with a newer writer. The established, well-known author lends his or her name to a project and offers work and guidance. The name and reputation of the established author can help sell the project to a publisher, or attract a larger audience if the book is an indie publication. This link to the more famous author can give the newer writer a tremendous career break.

Why is this important? Consider the movies bearing the label, "Steven Spielberg Presents". The Spielberg brand on a project gives it his stamp of approval and draws attention to it. When a big name author helps a newer author by adding his or her brand name to a book, it shines a spotlight on the less-known author.

Science fiction author Anne McCaffrey helped launch the careers of numerous young and talented authors via the Master and Apprentice method. Many of her junior coauthors went on to become award-winning or *New York Times* bestselling authors themselves. Anne often co-wrote in universes she had already established with her solo novels. Partnering with a junior writer allowed her to continue the series, build readership, and introduce her fans to other authors she thought they would enjoy. She and the junior author developed an outline or proposal for a new book. After Anne approved it, the Apprentice wrote the complete draft. Anne would make comments, give suggestions, brainstorm solutions to weak spots she found, and mentor the writer until the novel was acceptable to her. The books were published with her name and the newer writer's name on the cover.

Kevin receives more invitations to write short stories for commissioned anthologies than he can possibly write. Rather than turning them down, he often uses them as opportunities to present one of his writing students to a wider audience. He usually uses the First Draft, Final Draft method in the Master and Apprentice format. After they talk about the story—which might be about, say, purple unicorns or a spinoff story for the Planet of the Apes movie franchise—the junior writer writes the first draft. Then Kevin works on it and polishes it until it's ready to go. The Apprentice author gets a short story sale and credit, Kevin keeps the anthology editors happy, and the two authors split the money. Everyone benefits.

A common pitfall in this scenario is that the publisher may try to leave off the junior coauthor's name or drastically reduce the type size. Anne McCaffrey always insisted on giving the junior author full credit alongside her own name, and Kevin does the same, although he sometimes loses the battle about type size.

Frank Herbert, well-known author of *Dune*, had sold a contract for a book called *The Jesus Incident*, but because of other deadlines and complications in his life, as well as certain problems with the project, he saw the project delivery date looming and knew he couldn't do what he had promised. One of his good friends was the talented writer and award-winning Pacific Northwest poet, Bill Ransom. Frank and Bill often discussed writing.

Finally, during his deadline crisis, Frank went to Bill's house, knocked on the door, and asked, "Can you write like me?"

Herbert and Ransom collaborated on *The Jesus Incident* plus two sequels, *The Lazarus Effect* and *The Ascension Factor*. *The Jesus Incident* is widely considered a classic, one of Herbert's best. Because Frank Herbert was so well established, the publisher did not want a coauthor on the cover. Frank put his foot down, so the publisher agreed but retaliated by reducing his advance. Even so, Frank stuck to his guns. Fortunately the book sold extremely well, so the authors made money anyway. After that experience, Bill Ransom went on to write and publish three very well received science fiction novels of his own: *Jaguar*, *Viravax*, and *Burn*.

Similarly, the last novel that Frank Herbert published in his lifetime was a collaboration with his son Brian, *Man of Two Worlds*. At the time, Brian was an established and successful writer on his own, but Frank Herbert was a giant in the field and had often given his son writing advice and critiqued his manuscripts. When Brian originally set out to write *Man of Two Worlds* as a solo novel, Frank made extensive suggestions and eventually offered to write scenes and chapters, introducing a whole new set of characters. In his introduction to the thirtieth anniversary edition of *Man of Two Worlds*, Brian talks about the experience and describes how much he learned from working so closely with his father.

Many Padawan authors grow so successful that they become Masters and take on Apprentices of their own to coauthor books. Jody Lynn Nye, one of Anne McCaffrey's Apprentice writers, established a highly successful solo career and also wrote books with *New York Times* bestselling author Robert Asprin. Now, as a *New York Times* bestselling author in her own right, Jody has begun collaborations with some of her writing students.

Ghostwriting

Ghostwriters are hired to write much or all of the material for someone else, who is credited as the author. In most cases, the ghostwriter is a silent partner who receives little to no credit for the project. The credited author may have excellent complementary skills or may decide not to participate in the writing process at all.

The benefits of taking on such a project are

different from a collaboration in which people put their heads together to see what sort of wonderful creation they can produce. Writers need to make a living, and ghostwriting can pay quite well. A ghostwriter might not get the glory, but the income may cover the mortgage and the car payment. This form of collaboration can also be a tremendous learning experience in developing a writer's craft while still earning a paycheck.

Even before Kevin's first novel was published, he made a living as a technical writer for the Lawrence Livermore National Laboratory. He edited scientific papers, crafted presentations for technical conferences, and wrote textbooks on respirator safety and chemical protective clothing. In most of these cases he served as the equivalent of a ghostwriter. Occasionally he was recognized on the acknowledgments page, but authorship credit on the cover went to the scientist(s) who had done the research, whether or not they could write.

A ghostwriting project may involve someone who is renowned for a skill other than writing, like a politician, athlete, actor, or other celebrity. These individuals often have a large following of fans who want to read their books. Think of all the celebrity autobiographies—most of which probably weren't written by the celebrities themselves. In many cases, they shared their thoughts and stories in conversation, while the ghostwriter took notes, recorded the words, and crafted those ideas into a book "written by" that celebrity. Sometimes these ghostwriters are credited on the cover with phrases like "with Kevin J. Anderson" or "as told to Rebecca Moesta" in small letters under the celebrity's big name. But ghostwriters are often required to sign a nondisclosure agreement that prevents them from ever admitting that they authored the book.

We have both done ghostwriting projects. We learned from them, produced books we were proud of, cashed the checks, and moved on.

In one case, a celebrity came up with a concept for a young adult series. It was a paragraph long plus some bullet points, and Rebecca was hired to develop it and write it. The book came out under the celebrity's name, and we were sworn to secrecy. In another instance, a well-known research scientist wrote a novel centered around his highly topical work. It was relevant, with very thought-provoking science, but the plotting was problematic and the characters tissue thin. The publisher wanted to buy the novel, which showcased the celebrity's area of expertise, but only on the condition that the scientist hire an established author to rewrite the manuscript and make it publishable. He found Kevin, who took the rough draft, put it through a rigorous boot camp, and delivered a good book that served everyone's purposes. The novel was released under the scientist's name and Kevin was mentioned prominently in the acknowledgments.

In some cases, a successful author simply doesn't want to continue a series anymore, or maybe the author dies and the publisher wants more books in the popular series. Probably the best-known example of this is horror writer V.C. Andrews, who wrote the classic *Flowers in the Attic* and several sequels. After V.C. Andrews died in 1986, the estate hired another established author to write new novels under the name V.C. Andrews. Soon enough everyone realized that someone else was writing as "V.C. Andrews™," and eventually it was revealed to be Andrew Niederman, a respected horror author in his own right.

So if getting credit isn't of utmost importance to you and you can leave your ego at the door, think of yourself as a sort of surrogate mother who must give up the baby to the original parents. Then you may do well with ghostwriting.

Sandboxing

Sandboxing (which overlaps with Master and Apprentice) is working in someone else's universe. This is often work for hire. You sign a contract and agree to play in someone else's sandbox *with their toys*. This kind of writing requires flexibility and patience. It can be challenging for Pantsers, since writing a thorough outline is mandatory, and the Sandbox owner must approve it before you begin writing. (This can be a bit like collaborating with a committee.)

The owner of the universe or Sandbox has the first and final say. Some owners are easy to work with and some seem capricious. When the manuscript is written, the owner must again approve it or request changes. At any point, the owner can have a change of mind and ask for rewrites—even for parts of the manuscript that you thought were "approved" already.

The Sandbox owner keeps a percentage (often the lion's share). Remember that their brand name is usually responsible for selling the project to the public, so this is not unreasonable.

No matter how well known or unknown you are as an author, if you agree to work in someone else's sandbox, always remember whose toys you're playing with. Treat the owners, the readers, and the toys with respect. Do your best work with the material and resources you are given.

If the terms of Sandboxing sound unfair, depressing, or intolerable to you, we suggest you steer well clear of this type of collaboration.

Buddy System

Two or more collaborators gather in the same room and write interactively. One of the partners usually sits at the computer and types the manuscript as they work.

Jigsaw (a.k.a. Cat Wrangling)

In this method, multiple authors write stories, articles, or parts of the whole, and one of the partners fits all of the pieces together and edits them into a cohesive work. Jigsaw is often used for "braided" novels (a multi-POV book that follows several storylines that are separate but related) or shared universes (e.g., Wild Cards or Thieves' World).

Hybrid

Many of these methods can be combined or tweaked to make them work better to suit your particular collaboration.

CHAPTER 4

DECISIONS, PROBLEM-SOLVING, AND TIPS (WHAT?)

Once you pick your collaborator and decide on a method to use, you'll talk about the characters and the story. You'll make a grand plan. You'll imagine wild success. This will be the start of a beautiful relationship. What could possibly go wrong?

Plenty. It's always best to be frank and discuss difficult scenarios with your coauthor before tempers flare and blood pressure rises. When a conflict escalates it often becomes personal, which makes it harder to discuss rationally. Better to consider problems and brainstorm solutions while they are still theoretical.

DECISIONS, DECISIONS

Before you dive in, make a thorough agreement in writing. Discuss and agree on answers to these questions:

What kind of project is it?

Fiction, nonfiction, self-help? Script, story, treatment, novel, memoir? Boil it down to your elevator pitch. If possible, make an outline. Which rights do you plan to sell? (Publication, film/TV, game, sequel, stage, radio, merchandising?)

What are the limits of the collaboration?

Which ideas, notes, etc., belong to the project and which don't? Which rights may each of the partners exercise individually? Sequels, prequels, or competitive works? Do any rejected ideas, characters, and scenes belong to the partner who proposed them?

What are each partner's personal goals? What defines a project's success?

Publication, fame, wealth, critical recognition, personal satisfaction, fulfillment of a lifelong dream, producing literature, entertaining readers, changing the world. The list of possible goals is long. It's helpful if the partners have at least *some* goals in common.

How will the writing process work?

Will one partner write the narrative, and the other one flesh out dialogue and descriptions? Will you each write your draft chapters and then swap them for edits? Will you write close together or apart? Will you meet during the writing process? If so, how often and how will you meet? What does each partner need to do to meet his or her obligations? (e.g., If you decide to use the First Draft, Final Draft method the division of labor might seem obvious. But what if you spend months writing the first draft of the book and your coauthor just skims it in a few days and says "Sure, looks fine to me." Does that really fulfill your expectations of the collaboration?)

How will editing or critiquing work?

Will you discuss these out loud? Make edits in the electronic files? Use a comments function in your software? This can be a tricky balance. The longer you work together, the easier it gets.

What is the schedule for completion?

Agree on a schedule and deadlines, but don't expect a best-case scenario. Allow up to twice the amount of time you would have expected the project to take. Unless the project is sold to an outside entity that imposes a strict deadline, don't be hard-nosed about the schedule. And don't make missing a deadline into a breach of contract.

What are the ownership percentages?

In many cases, all partners own equal shares in a jointly created work, but not always. Don't take the percentages for granted. Specify them in writing.

How will you split the income?

For authors at a comparable level in their careers, the usual answer is to split the money evenly. But there are many other scenarios:

- If one of the collaborators brings fame or higher earning potential to the table, that partner might want and deserve a larger percentage of the income. The more junior author still benefits by getting a higher rate of pay than by working alone, increasing name recognition, having association with the more famous author, getting a pro sale, etc.
- If one partner had the original idea, consider giving that partner a majority interest (e.g., 51/49 percent for two partners, or 34/33/33 percent for three).
- If one partner owns the underlying rights (such as in an established

intellectual property), the split may be much larger for that partner.
- If one partner participates in more of the public appearances, consider allocating a larger proportion of the sales at those events to that partner.

How will money be collected and paid out?

Do you share the same agent? Does one author receive the payment directly and then cut a check to the other author? Or does the publisher divide the money and send separate checks to the authors or their agents?

How will the copyright be held?

Decide how the copyright will be registered: under all names, under only some of the partners' names, under a pen name, under the name of a corporation, etc.

Who gets credit and how?

Will each partner's name appear on the work and in what order? Will credits be listed as A and B, A with B, A presents B, or A as told to B? Will the partners use a pseudonym?

Who will represent the project?

If each of you has an agent, attorney, or manager, which individual is going to market the project? How will commissions be split? If the agents disagree, how will the disagreement be resolved?

How will you handle the dedication and acknowledgments?

Does everyone get to include a dedication for the book? Do you:

- Split the dedication page, so that each contributor gets to dedicate?
- Mutually agree on one person or group to dedicate the book to?

- Only allow one author to dedicate the book? If so, why? (Seniority? Level of contribution? Project ownership?)

Does everyone get to include people to thank in the acknowledgments? Do you:

- Split the acknowledgments page, so that each contributor gets a section?
- Combine all of the acknowledgments for all collaborators on one page?

How will you handle expenses?

If one or more partners pay for research, cover art, editing, design, additional proofreading, or marketing, do those individuals recoup their expenses before income is divided? Or should all partners simply split expenses? Do all partners have to agree on an expense for it to be reimbursed?

How will you divide any non-writing responsibilities?

Assign individual tasks. Who will hire editors or designers, negotiate contracts, field interviews, and handle social media? Don't blithely assume all responsibilities will be shared equally. You may find a magical collaboration in which the partners do this, but don't count on it. People have strengths and weaknesses, and we tend to avoid work we find unpleasant. Decide what is expected of each partner before something important falls through the cracks. Promotion can make or break a book. How will you divide the promotion and marketing work after publication? Do you each have a mailing list? A newsletter? An active social media presence?

What are the legal powers of each collaborator?

Do individual partners have the power to sell or license the work without the other partner's consent (whether or not income would be shared)? Or does only one senior or originating partner have that right? You may want to agree that no partner may transfer, sell, or license, any interest in the project without consent of the other partner(s).

What are each collaborator's legal responsibilities?

Each partner should agree in writing that all work they contribute will be original, won't infringe on copyrights, won't be defamatory, and won't invade privacy or breach other rights. If you feel that a partner has contributed potentially problematic material, reject the material or rewrite it. In any case, if one of the partners violates these legal ground rules, that partner should cover costs and liabilities associated with the violation.

How will you handle disagreements?

There will be disagreements. Listen to and respect each other. Check your ego at the door and try to work toward the best result. If you can't come to a consensus, decide up front who will have the final say. The type of collaboration may affect how the decisions are made. There are many ways to address differences of opinion and to distribute problem-solving authority. If the project has a senior partner, typically that person decides. When we (Kevin and Rebecca) couldn't come to an agreement, we assigned jurisdiction based on areas of expertise. If the dispute had to do with plot or pacing, for example, Kevin had the final say. If it dealt with motivation or character development, Rebecca would make the final call. If you don't agree on which partner should make a choice, you could appoint a trusted mediator.

What constitutes the collaboration?

Specify the scope of the project(s) that the writers will collaborate on. (Usually you aren't forming a permanent business partnership.) If the partners finish the projects covered by the original agreement, it's relatively easy to make a new agreement that is similar. A new agreement can be a great opportunity to work out any kinks from a previous version of the collaboration contract.

How will death or disability be handled?

What if one partner falls off a mountain, gets hit by lightning, or can't continue writing? Does the remaining partner(s) continue the writing and split income and credit as before? Or does the remaining partner(s) have the right to finish the project and make a fair adjustment in credit, ownership, and income? Does all decision-making authority transfer to the remaining partner(s), or do the heirs or assigns of the deceased/disabled partner still have a vote?

How will you handle termination?

What if one of the partners wants to leave the project? Again, it's essential to cover the worst-case scenario. You may find that the collaboration doesn't work out. If you and your collaborator(s) part ways, what happens? Who owns the work? Who, if anyone, has the right to finish and sell the project?

How will you divide the work?

- By chapters or sections (e.g., random or specific; every other chapter)
- By storyline (geographic or subject or a/b/c storyline, e.g., all scenes with crystal mining, or all scenes involving the ship mutiny, or all scenes in Australia, or all scenes on Glarphon Prime)
- By character POV
- By subject-matter expertise (science, horses, country/language knowledge, medicine, sailing ships, or any other subject that one of the authors is more knowledgeable in)
- By preference (each author picks chapters they'd like to write the first draft of)
- By scene type (action sequences, romance, introspection, etc.)
- By function (one writes narrative, another fleshes out dialogue or scene descriptions)

COMMUNICATION

Like any relationship, a writing partnership thrives on respect and communication. In writing, some of the main areas of communication involve goal setting, division of labor, brainstorming, and editing.

Be respectful of each other's writing time. Talk about which communication methods work best for you and your coauthor and make good use of them. Which of these do you prefer:

- Phone calls
- Email
- In-person meetings
- Video chat
- Text messages
- Voicemail
- Snail mail (what—that still exists?)

The same goes for how you share files and important documents with each other. These are just a few examples of the software tools available:

- Email
- Dropbox

- Google Drive
- Hightail
- Microsoft OneDrive
- Slack

PROBLEM-SOLVING

"It was a beautiful friendship." If you decide to write a book with a close friend, be aware of the possible pitfalls. Just because you get along on everything else together doesn't mean that you'll be good writing partners. You need to be creatively in sync. You need to agree on the same vision for the book. We know of several severely broken friendships that occurred because of attempted collaboration.

A study on collaboration by Ede and Lunsford [see Reference 3] showed that the satisfaction level of authors in group writing projects was affected by eight factors:

1. How well goals are articulated and shared
2. The level of openness and mutual respect

3. How much control the writers have over the text
4. How much control the writers have when others modify the text
5. How credit is acknowledged
6. How conflicts are managed and disputes are resolved
7. The level of administrative restrictions imposed on the authors (e.g., external deadlines, NDAs, technical-legal requirements)
8. The perceived value of the project to the organization (e.g., the publisher)

Who has the final say? If you're following the Master and Apprentice method, the "boss" is usually obvious. If you're Stephen King's Padawan and he says the adverb stays, then the adverb stays.

But what if you are equally matched as writers? As collaborators, always play to your strengths. Not everybody is good at all facets of writing. But if you don't discuss this beforehand you might find resentment brewing. You could decide who the "boss" is based on your strengths, if they are clearly drawn. The science partner has the final say on technical or engineering questions; the historian can overrule any questions on period details. Or if one writer is acknowledged as the best plotter, the other might be the master character builder, so align decision making accordingly. Even when you are the boss, we'd advise you not to exercise the veto power too often. Try to negotiate in every possible case.

These tips can help you resolve some problems that may crop up:

- **Don't be a glory hog.** No matter what the division of labor is, don't claim all the credit. Give each other credit and use acknowledgments to thank everyone who helped any of the writing partners or otherwise contributed to the project.
- **Don't sweat the small stuff.** Keep your eye on the goal. For a collaboration to work, you have to be willing to give up some level of control. Don't butt heads over inconsequential issues. Pick your battles.
- **Don't fall into the mind-reading trap.** You and your writing

partner(s) may think alike on many issues, but don't expect him or her to know what you think without being told. If you want your collaborator to be aware of something, say it in a nice way or put it politely in writing. For example, "I sometimes use adverbs that end in -ly. I believe it's fine in moderation, so please don't edit them all out." Or "I'd like to use first person present tense for all four of the main POV characters. Can we try that?" Or "I work best late at night, so I don't wake up until noon. If you want to get a message to me in the morning, please text me or use email."

- **Leave your ego at the door.** Listen to your coauthor's suggestions and respect his or her opinion. You're raising this baby novel together, and sometimes you'll disagree on the parenting.

- **Focus on the story as paramount.** Remember that you and your coauthor(s) are trying to create something *together*, and in most cases, the finished product will credit each collaborator (not just you).

- **Don't get personal.** If you dislike part of a scene your partner wrote, don't complain about their dog, or children, or the fact that their house is a mess. Stay objective about the writing issue.
- **Learn how to share.**
- **Don't see your words as too precious to change.** Let it go.
- **There's no single "right" way** to go about the process of writing with partners. Use the collaborative system that works best for *your* writing team.
- **Editing online, instead of on paper, can be helpful**. Don't use Markup or Track Changes. This way the rewrites remain invisible to you and your coauthor and produce less friction.

GRATITUDE

No writer is an "island". This should be especially clear when you collaborate. Give thanks and compliment your partner when he or she does something good. For example, "Hey, that scene you wrote with Lt. Rykk on the beach as the tsunami approached was really good. I was practically biting my nails." Or "Thanks for your suggestion about how to build suspense when the blind girl arrived. It helped a lot, and I wrote that chapter in record time!"

Expressing your sincere thanks is a morale booster for everyone involved.

You'll never lose stature in the eyes of your readers by being grateful, either. In fact, they will probably respect you more.

It's healthy for you to spend some time remembering how many people contribute to successfully writing and publishing a book. A little bit of appreciation goes a long way. So make liberal use of the acknowledgments section in your book. Be specific about why you are thanking people.

Examples of people to thank:

- Family
- Friends
- Assistants/support staff
- Bosses
- Coworkers
- Editors
- Publishers
- First readers
- Agents
- Researchers
- Sources
- Mentors
- Teachers
- Inspirations
- Supportive organizations
- Sponsors or contributors

CHAPTER 5

WORST-CASE SCENARIOS

Let's be pragmatic and look at some worst-case scenarios. Each individual case has its own solution or set of solutions. Sometimes the only way out may be just to abandon the project and cling to the lessons learned. In a worst-case scenario, questions can come up that you might not have considered beforehand. Here are some examples.

Let's say you have a great idea for a series of dragon rodeo adventures. In your excitement, you talk to your best friend Marcy about it. She gets just as excited, tossing in some excellent suggestions, a whole storyline, and before you know it, you've decided to collaborate. Once Marcy added her input, which became vital to the series, the dragon rodeo series was no longer just "your" idea.

But as you work together, the two of you run into problems. You're a Plotter and Marcy is a Pantser. In your vision, the series of young adult adventures features a scamp who runs away from his ranch and joins the rodeo because he loves dragons. Marcy, however, envisions the series as adult thrillers featuring one of the dragon rodeo clowns who solves mysteries in the towns where the rodeo travels. Soon, you two have irreconcilable differences and the whole dragon rodeo project crashes and burns. Although you and Marcy manage to stay friends, you're never going to write that series in collaboration.

Okay, so who owns that idea? You came up with the "dragon rodeo" concept in the first place, but you shared it with Marcy. She contributed vital ideas. The two of you brainstormed and developed it together. Can *you* just go off and write your dragon rodeo series as you originally envisioned it, while Marcy independently writes her thriller series featuring the dragon rodeo clown? Probably not. The projects might seem too similar and the high concept would be diluted. You could negotiate a buy-out for one or the other of you, flip a coin, arm wrestle. Or the only solution might be just to abandon the idea and come up with another one.

Here's a slightly different scenario. Let's say you and Marcy do write the dragon rodeo series together. You sell the books to a major publisher, or decide to indie publish them together. The first book comes out and is very successful. Then Marcy is in a car accident and is unable to complete her part of the second book. In fact, she may not be in a position to go back to writing for a year or more. But the series is just taking off, and readers are already clamoring for the next installment. You signed the contract for the second book before Marcy's accident, and the publisher is already promoting it. What do you do?

For Kevin and Brian's Dune novels, they agreed in advance that if anything should happen to either of them, the other writer would complete the project under contract, and they would split the money as originally agreed. This solid, trusting partnership has worked well for them since the late 1990s. They trust each other to hold up their end of the agreement. They also know that personal disasters can happen to anyone, and circumstances can arise in which one of them might not be able to complete the work, no matter how much they may want to. In cases like that, they have each other's backs.

But what if Marcy just flaked out? What if she decided to become a basket weaver at folk fairs and not do any more writing, leaving you high and dry? You complete the novel or series by yourself. Then how would you determine how the money was divided? Who owns the series? Are you allowed just to keep writing more books on your own? Would Marcy keep getting credit—and payment—even if she stopped co-writing them?

What if Marcy died? Do her heirs then get a creative say in what you do with the series? Would you really want Cousin Jennie (who "always wanted to be a writer") to be able to tell you how to plot the next book? Or does the right to make future creative decisions on the property revert to you?

Here's another possible wrinkle: Say you and Marcy create the successful dragon rodeo series and write several books together. What if *you* lose interest and you want to move on and write other things? Marcy though, loves the series and wants to keep writing them. If she goes solo in your collaborative series, how would the money be split on future volumes and how would the author credit be handled? Kevin and his past coauthors decided that in such cases the continuing author would receive 75 percent and the co-creator of the series would get 25 percent.

Whichever way you and your partner decide to resolve this, it's best to think of the situation *beforehand*, when the conflict is still theoretical.

What if you and Marcy have written some books together and then bring in another collaborator down the road? One way might be for the first two authors to be listed as "creators" and the new writer to get a byline and an appropriate share of the book—but not of the underlying intellectual property.

What if a movie or TV series is made of the dragon rodeo books after Marcy abandons the series, or after you've brought on a third partner?

Admittedly, some of these decisions may be complex, and solutions may need to be worked out in detail with attorneys. These are just examples of ways that something can go wrong, even when the series is a success.

A collaboration agreement does not imply that you don't trust each other. It's an acknowledgement of the worst-case scenarios that could come up, and it provides a written record of your mutual understanding. In the appendix to this book, we've included a sample generic collaboration agreement that you can use or adapt to meet your needs.

SUMMARY

Writing doesn't have to be a solitary activity. You can share the work and your imagination to create a rewarding synergy. Some of the world's finest examples of creativity have come from two people joining their heads, hearts, and souls together to produce wonderful works of art.

Kevin switches easily between writing solo novels and collaborative novels, and continues to do both, with many bestselling books of each kind. But if you've always been a solitary writer, it's a big shift. Opening your mind and your words to someone else is more challenging than just learning to share a bathroom. It's like getting married, agreeing on how to raise the children, then actually doing it.

Not a simple process, but so worthwhile when it succeeds.

Approach collaboration with your eyes wide open. Be prepared and be realistic. Know the advantages, the methods, and the risks. You may want to start by trying it just for fun, as a learning experience. Every writer's technique is different, and by working together on a creative project you both can learn and grow as authors. Eventually your collaboration may become a successful and lucrative writing arrangement.

We've participated in many wonderful collaborative partnerships that produced books we're immensely proud of, books we never could have written on our own. Our experiences collaborating with each other have been powerful and rewarding.

Think about it. Look around for a compatible writer. Try a story together. Lean on each other's strengths and shore up each other's weaknesses.

Writing can be a team sport.

REFERENCES

1. Lowry, Paul Benjamin; Curtis, Aaron; Lowry, Michelle René (2004). "Building a Taxonomy and Nomenclature of Collaborative Writing to Improve Interdisciplinary Research and Practice." Journal of Business Communication. 41: 66.

2. Onrubia, Javier; Engle, Anna (2009). "Strategies for collaborative writing and phases of knowledge construction in CSCL environments." Computers & Education. 53 (4): 1256–1265.

3. Ede, L.; Lunsford, A. (1990). "Singular Text/Plural Authors: Perspectives on Collabora-

tive Authoring." Carbondale: Southern Illinois University Press.

SAMPLE COLLABORATION
AGREEMENT

THIS COLLABORATION AGREEMENT ("Agreement") is entered into and made effective on _____ (the "Effective Date") by and between Writer A ("Writer A"), with an address of 123 Main St., Anywhere, XY 00000 and Writer B ("Writer B"), PO Box 111, Somewhere, XZ 99999. Writer A and Writer B are each referred to in this Agreement as a "Party" and collectively as the "Parties."

WHEREAS, Writer A and Writer B desire to co-author a joint work [insert brief description];

NOW, THEREFORE, in consideration of the mutual covenants set forth below, and other good and valuable consideration, the receipt and sufficiency of which is hereby acknowledged, the Parties agree as follows:

1. Obligations. The Parties agree to work together in good faith to perform the obligations under this Agreement between the Parties and with any designated publisher for the Work, including meeting deadlines and providing any edits or approvals to the publisher in a timely manner.

2. Acknowledgments.
2.1. The Work is a stand-alone project. Nothing contained in the Agreement shall be interpreted or construed to obligate Writer A and Writer B to co-create additional projects.
2.2. Nothing contained in the Agreement shall be interpreted or construed to grant to Writer A any rights, title or interest in or to any works or other intellectual property created by Writer B. Nothing contained in the Agreement shall be interpreted or construed to grant to Writer B any rights, title or interest in or to any works or other intellectual property created by Writer A.

3. Ownership. It is and has at all times been the intention of the Parties that they be joint creators

of the Work in equal shares. The copyrights in the Work shall be owned jointly by the Parties. In the event that it is determined that the contribution of one of the Parties to the Work is deemed to not meet the statutory requirements of copyrightability, the remaining Party hereby assigns an interest in the Work to the other Party, so that the Work shall be jointly owned by the Parties in equal shares. No Party may divide, sell, license or otherwise dispose of any rights in the Work without the prior written approval of the remaining Party. No license or other contract with respect to the Work shall be valid without the signature of both Parties.

4. Right to Publish. No Party may unilaterally enter into an agreement to divide, sell, license or otherwise dispose of any rights of publication of the Work without the prior written approval of both Parties. No Party may unilaterally self-publish the Work.

5. Publicity. The Parties may use portions of the Text(s) to promote and advertise the Work. The Parties will work together to limit complete exposure of the Text(s) and Work in and through publicity efforts.

6. Merchandising. No Party may unilaterally enter into an agreement to divide, sell, license or otherwise dispose of any rights of merchandising of the Work without the prior written approval of both Parties.

7. Royalties and Advances. The Parties shall share equally in all net royalties and advances paid in connection with the publication and sales of the Work and any license of any rights of the Work, including but not limited to electronic rights, audio rights, multimedia rights, foreign language rights, and reprint and special edition rights. If agreeable with the publisher, all agreements for publication and sale of the Work and for the license of any rights in the Work shall provide that each Party shall be paid its equal share directly (or to such Party's agent, if so designated). Parties acknowledge publisher may be unwilling or unable to pay one-half shares directly, and agree that the Parties will work together to designate a receiver to collect and distribute the monies in the manner and time agreed by Parties.

8. Representations and Warranties.

8.1. Writer A hereby represents, warrants and agrees that: (a) Writer A will cooperate with Writer B in the preparation of the Work; and (b) all text furnished by Writer A for use in the Work will be wholly original with Writer A, will not be copied in whole or in part from any work, will not violate, conflict with or infringe upon any personal or property rights whatsoever of any person or entity, including without limitation, any copyright, trademark or other proprietary right of others and contain no matter that is libelous, an invasion of privacy or infringement upon the copyright, trademark or other intellectual property rights of any person or entity, or be otherwise unlawful. The representations and warranties made by Writer A in this paragraph and the indemnity obligations, shall survive the termination for any reason of this Agreement.

8.2. Writer B hereby represents, warrants and agrees that: (a) Writer B will cooperate with Writer A in the preparation of the Work; and (b) all text furnished by Writer B for use in the Work will be wholly original with Writer B, will not be copied in whole or in part from any work, will not violate, conflict with or infringe upon any personal or property rights whatsoever of any person or entity, including without limitation, any copyright, trademark or other proprietary right of others and contain no matter that is libelous, an invasion of privacy or infringement upon the copyright, trademark or other intellectual property rights of any person or entity, or be otherwise unlawful. The representations and warranties made by Writer B in this paragraph and the indemnity obligations, shall survive the termination for any reason of this Agreement.

9. <u>Copyright</u>. Publisher shall register the Work in the name of Writer A and Writer B with the United States Copyright Office. All parties shall execute such documents as may be necessary to effectuate copyright of the Work in accordance with the Agreement.

10. <u>Credits</u>. Contingent upon a publisher agreement, Writer B and Writer A will receive credit as co-author of the Text. Co-author credit will appear on the Cover and the Title Page of each Work.

11. <u>Indemnification</u>.
11.1. With regard to the portions of the Work

contributed by Writer A, Writer A shall defend, indemnify and hold Writer B harmless from and against any losses, liabilities, damages, settlements, costs and expenses (including reasonable attorneys' fees) arising out of or for the purpose of avoiding any suit, proceeding, claim or demand or the settlement thereof, which may be brought or made against Writer B by reason of (i) the publication, sale, or distribution of the Works of the Work based on those portions of the Work contributed by Writer A, or (ii) a breach or alleged breach by Writer A of any of the representations and warranties.

11.2. With regard to the portions of the Work contributed by Writer B, Writer B shall defend, indemnify and hold Writer A harmless from and against any losses, liabilities, damages, settlements, costs and expenses (including reasonable attorneys' fees) arising out of or for the purpose of avoiding any suit, proceeding, claim or demand or the settlement thereof, which may be brought or made against Writer A by reason of (i) the publication, sale, or distribution of the Works of the Work based on those portions of the Work contributed by Writer B, or (ii) a breach or alleged breach by Writer B of any of the representations and warranties. Such indemnification shall apply notwithstanding the fact that any portion of the Work contributed by Writer B, has been reviewed and/or approved by Writer A.

12. Term. The term of this Agreement shall be for the life of the copyrights of the Works.

13. Expenses. Writer A and Writer B shall each be responsible for their own expenses incurred in connection with the performance of this Agreement; however, the commissions and expenses owed [Agent] as literary agent in this Agreement shall be shared equally by Writer B and Writer A.

14. Miscellaneous. This Agreement constitutes the entire agreement between Writer A and Writer B and supersedes all prior agreements, understandings and proposals (whether oral or written) concerning the subject matter of this Agreement. No waiver or modification of any provision hereunder shall be binding unless in writing and signed by both Parties. No waiver of any breach hereof shall be construed to be a continuing waiver or consent to any subsequent breach hereof.

15. <u>Failure to Complete Collaborative Work(s).</u> In the event Writer B or Writer A is unable or unwilling to continue or complete any Work covered in this Agreement, the other Party may complete said Work(s) without the assistance or advice of the Party who is unable or unwilling to continue or complete the Work(s); provided, the rights of the withdrawing Party as to all matters under this Agreement, including the right to a share of monies received, credit and copyright, shall, in the absence of an agreement between the Parties, be determined based upon the amount, substantiality and value of the withdrawing Party's contribution to the Work(s) in relation to the contributions and the continuing responsibilities to the Work(s) by the remaining Party.

16. <u>Death or Disability.</u>
16.1. This Agreement shall inure to the benefit of, and shall be binding upon, each party's respective executors, administrators, heirs, successors and assigns.
16.2. In the event of the death or disability of a Party before or after the Work as defined in this Agreement is completed, the surviving or non-disabled Party shall have the sole and unrestricted

right to complete the Works covered in this Agreement, alone or in conjunction with others, and thereafter to publish said Work(s); provided, the rights of the deceased or disabled Party as to all matters under this Agreement, including the right to a share of monies received, credit and copyright, shall be determined based upon the amount, substantiality and value of the deceased or disabled Party's contribution to the Work(s) in relation to the contributions and the continuing responsibilities to the Work(s) by the remaining Party. The surviving or non-disabled Party shall have the sole and unrestricted right to make all literary, editorial and business decisions with respect to the Work and to execute all documents necessary to sell or license any right of the Work.

16.3. Upon timely request, copies of all licenses and other agreements executed in connection with the Work as defined by this Agreement, as well as copies of all royalty and accounting statements received by the surviving or non-disabled Parties in connection with this Agreement, shall be furnished in a timely manner to the deceased or disabled Party's executor or other representative.

16.4. The deceased or disabled Party shall retain credit as co-author of the Works covered in this

Agreement and shall retain status as co-owner of the copyright for the Works completed jointly by Writer B and Writer A. The deceased or disabled Party shall continue to share equally with the surviving or non-disabled Party the monies received for Works completed jointly by Writer B and Writer A.

16.5. The deceased or disabled Party shall share proportionally with the surviving or non-disabled Party the monies received for the Works in progress by Writer B and Writer A and completed by the surviving or non-disabled Party—the proportion based on the amount, substantiality and value of the deceased or disabled Party's contribution to the Works completed by the surviving or non-disabled Party.

17. <u>Governing Law and Venue</u>. This Collaboration Agreement shall be governed by the laws of the State of [State] without reference to conflicts of law principles. The Parties hereby consent that the venue for any action on this Collaboration Agreement shall be _____ [State].

18. <u>Severability</u>. If and to the extent that any provision of this Agreement is held to be illegal, invalid,

or unenforceable, in whole or in part, such provision or such portion thereof shall be ineffective as to the jurisdiction in which it is illegal, invalid or unenforceable to the extent of its illegality, invalidity or unenforceability and shall be deemed modified to the extent necessary to conform to applicable law so as to give the maximum effect to the intent of the Parties. The illegality, invalidity, or unenforceability of such provision in that jurisdiction shall not in any way affect the legality, validity, or enforceability of any other provision of this Agreement in any other jurisdiction. This Agreement is the entire agreement between the Parties with respect to the subject matter herein, and this Agreement may only be amended by written instrument executed by all Parties.

IN WITNESS WHEREOF, the Parties have caused this Agreement to be executed as of _____ [Effective Date].

ACCEPTED AND AGREED:
   [signature lines]

ABOUT THE AUTHORS

Kevin J. Anderson has published 150 books, fifty-six of which were national or international bestsellers. He has written numerous novels in the Star Wars, X-Files, Dune, and DC Comics universes, as well as unique steampunk fantasy novels *Clockwork Angels* and *Clockwork Lives*, written with legendary rock drummer Neil Peart, based on the concept album by the band Rush. His original works include the Saga of Seven Suns series, the Terra Incognita fantasy trilogy, the Saga of Shadows trilogy, and his humorous horror series featuring Dan Shamble, Zombie PI. Kevin has edited numerous anthologies, written comics and games, and the lyrics to two rock CDs. He has collaborated with dozens of different coauthors, including his wife of more than a quarter century, Rebecca Moesta. He and Rebecca are the publishers of WordFire Press.

Rebecca Moesta (pronounced MESS-tuh) is the bestselling author of forty books, both solo and in collaboration with her husband, Kevin J. Anderson. Her solo work includes novels in the *Buffy the Vampire Slayer* and *Junior Jedi Knights* series, short stories, articles, ghostwriting, and editing anthologies. With Kevin, she has written the *Crystal Doors* trilogy, the *Star Challengers* trilogy, the *Young Jedi Knights* series, movie and game novelizations, lyrics for rock CDs, graphic novels, pop-up books, and writing books, such as *Million Dollar Professionalism for Writers*.

Rebecca and Kevin are the publishers of WordFire Press. For more about them, see wordfire.com

IF YOU LIKED THIS BOOK

Million Dollar Productivity by Kevin J. Anderson

Million Dollar Professionalism by Kevin J. Anderson and Rebecca Moesta

Worldbuilding: From Small Towns to Entire Universes by Kevin J. Anderson

OTHER WORDFIRE PRESS TITLES

by Kevin J. Anderson and Rebecca Moesta

Crystal Doors #1: Island Realm
Crystal Doors #2: Ocean Realm
Crystal Doors #3: Sky Realm

Star Challengers #1: Moonbase Crisis
Star Challengers #2: Space Station Crisis
Star Challengers #3: Asteroid Crisis

www.ingramcontent.com/pod-product-compliance
Lightning Source LLC
Chambersburg PA
CBHW060533080526
44586CB00012B/716